THE BEST OF
CALIFORNIA

THE BEST OF
CALIFORNIA
A COOKBOOK

Ann Walker & Larry Walker

Food Photography by Steven Mark Needham

CollinsPublishersSanFrancisco
A Division of HarperCollins*Publishers*

First published in USA 1994 by CollinsPublishersSanFrancisco
1160 Battery Street, San Francisco, CA 94111

Produced by Smallwood and Stewart, Inc.,
New York City

© 1994 Smallwood and Stewart, Inc.

Editor: Kathy Kingsley
Food Styling: Ann Disrude
Prop Styling: Bette Blau

Photography credits: Robert Holmes: 1; 2–3; 41; 47; 69.
Michael J. Howell/Picture Perfect USA: 33.
John W. Warden/Picture Perfect USA: 7; 75.

Library of Congress Cataloging-in-Publication Data
Walker, Ann,
       The best of California : a cookbook /
Ann and Larry Walker : food photography
by Steven Mark Needham.
       p. cm.
Includes index.
ISBN 0-00-255478-X
1. Cookery, American—California style.
I. Walker, Larry, II. Title.
TX715.2.C34W35   1994
641.59794—dc20   93-43040
                                                          CIP

Printed in China

Contents

Introduction

California's history has forever been shaped by newcomers, and nowhere is this more true than in the wonderful culinary kaleidoscope known as California cuisine. The early Spanish missionaries established an agricultural base, introducing fruit trees, chile peppers, olives, and grapevines, all of which still play a significant role in local cooking. Later settlers discovered gold in the mid-19th century, and the waves of immigrants that followed – Italians, French, Portuguese, Germans, Spanish, Irish, Japanese, and Chinese – brought a different kind of treasure with them: Collectively they created a cuisine of almost unparalleled diversity.

Because of these immigrants, the roots of California cuisine are remarkably international, reaching from the Mediterranean to Asia, pushing north from Mexico and Latin America, and are nourished by an abundant supply of excellent ingredients: plentiful and varied seafood from the north coast; all kinds of fresh produce, coaxed by

irrigation from the Central Valley and the Salinas Valley in Monterey County; fruits and nuts from the orchards and groves of the San Joaquin Valley and the south; and meat from the state's cattle ranches.

But it wasn't until the 1960s and early 1970s that this smorgasbord of culinary richness began to take shape as an important world cuisine, sparked by the enthusiasm and skill of such chefs as Alice Waters (Chez Panisse and Café Fanny in Berkeley), Jeremiah Tower (Stars Restaurant in San Francisco and Oakville, Napa Valley), and Michael Wild (Bay Wolf in Oakland). Most important was their demand for only the freshest and most natural ingredients. They encouraged local producers not only to stop using pesticides and herbicides but also to cultivate or seek out varieties of fruits and vegetables with the best flavors. Out of this grew a proliferation of farmers' markets throughout the state, providing outlets for hundreds of dedicated small producers and offering a dizzying variety of fresh produce.

At the same time, California wines also gained international acclaim, enhancing and encouraging the new cuisine. Napa and Sonoma counties, just north of San Francisco, are the best known wine-growing areas, but world-class wines are being made from Mendocino County in the north to the Temecula Valley in the south.

California's reputation has been built by fine Cabernet Sauvignon, Chardonnay, Pinot Noir, Sauvignon Blanc, and Zinfandel.

Today, bountiful fresh produce is still the foundation of the well-stocked California kitchen, along with a good supply of basic Mediterranean herbs and spices, including garlic, basil, rosemary, sage, and thyme; Asian specialties such as coriander seeds, ginger root, star anise, Thai basil, and fermented fish sauce; and fresh cilantro and a selection of chiles, both fresh and dried, from Latin American markets. California cooks love to put together ingredients seldom found elsewhere in the same kitchen, let alone the same cooking pot ~ ingredients from Asia and Mexico, for example ~ to create startling but delicious combinations of flavors.

As might be expected in the state that is home to Hollywood, imagination is more important than rules or recipes. In California there has always been a willingness to experiment. In that spirit, we urge you to use these recipes as guides, not as absolute commands. Bring your own skills and sense of adventure to the recipes, modify them, and serve them as you wish. That is, after all, true to the California style.

Larry and Ann Walker

Barbecued Tomales Bay Oysters
with Anchovy Sauce

Tomales Bay, about 40 miles north of San Francisco, is best known for its oyster farming. One of our favorite ways to enjoy the plentiful shellfish is barbecued. For this recipe, use small oysters, such as Pacifics or Hog Island Sweetwaters.

Anchovy Sauce:

¼ cup (½ stick) unsalted butter, softened

¼ cup olive oil

6 anchovy fillets, drained & chopped

1 small garlic clove, minced

¼ cup grated aged Asiago or Parmesan cheese

¼ teaspoon black pepper

2 tablespoons fresh lemon juice

½ teaspoon hot-pepper sauce

4 dozen small oysters

Prepare the sauce: In a small bowl, using the back of a spoon, mash together the butter, olive oil, anchovies, garlic, cheese, and pepper until the mixture forms a paste. Stir in the lemon juice and hot-pepper sauce. Set aside.

Prepare a fire in a kettle-type charcoal grill. When the coals are burning white, spread them evenly over the bottom of the grill. Place the rack on the grill and put the oysters on the rack, rounded side down. Close the lid, leaving the vents open. Grill for 10 to 15 minutes, or until the shells have opened slightly. Remove the oysters from the grill and pry off the top shells. Return the oysters in their bottom shells to the grill. Spoon a small amount of the sauce on each oyster. Close the lid of the grill and cook for 2 minutes more, or until the sauce is melted and warm. Serve immediately. **Serves 8 to 12.**

Quesadillas

These stuffed tortillas are one of many Mexican contributions to the California table. Cut into wedges, quesadillas are the perfect quick bite for unexpected guests or hungry children. The traditional filling is simply a mild cheese, but our California-style version and variation should inspire you to create even more of your own.

*1 canned chile chipotle
  in adobo sauce*

1 cup shredded Swiss cheese

6 ounces cream cheese, softened

Twelve 8-inch flour tortillas

*6 ounces smoked turkey breast,
  thinly sliced*

*2 to 3 tablespoons vegetable
  or olive oil*

Preheat the oven to 200°F.

In a food processor fitted with the metal blade, combine the chile, Swiss cheese, and cream cheese, and process until smooth.

Lay 1 tortilla on a work surface. Spread a thin layer of the cheese mixture over the tortilla and cover with a layer of turkey. Top with another tortilla. Set aside. Repeat with the remaining ingredients.

In a medium-size skillet, heat 1 teaspoon of the oil over medium heat. Transfer 1 quesadilla to the skillet and cook for 1 minute, or until the underside is golden. Using a spatula, turn it over and cook for 1 minute more, or until the underside is golden. Remove to paper towels to drain, then transfer to a heatproof plate and keep warm in the oven. Cook the remaining quesadillas, adding more oil to the skillet as necessary. Cut each quesadilla into 8 wedges and serve warm. **Serves 6 to 12.**

Goat Cheese, Mango & Shrimp Filling: In a medium-size bowl, mash 4 ounces goat cheese and 4 ounces cream cheese with a fork.

Peel, seed, and thinly slice 1 large ripe mango. Spread a thin layer of the cheese mixture over 1 tortilla. Scatter 2 tablespoons peeled tiny shrimp evenly over the cheese. Sprinkle with ¼ teaspoon fresh lime juice.

Cover the shrimp with a layer of mango slices, then top with another tortilla. Repeat with the remaining ingredients and cook the quesadillas as directed.

Steamed Purple Potatoes with Sour Cream and Salmon Caviar

This dramatic appetizer not only tastes sensational but is visually spectacular as well. Purple potatoes, which originated in Peru, have been warmly received in the California kitchen. They resemble small russets but have dark skin and a bright purple interior. If you can't find the purple variety, you can substitute red-skinned new potatoes.

8 small purple potatoes, about 1½ to 2 inches long

1 teaspoon salt

5 to 6 tablespoons sour cream

3 tablespoons salmon caviar

Fill a medium-size saucepan with 2 inches of water. Set the potatoes on a steamer in the pan and sprinkle with ½ teaspoon of the salt. Bring the water to a simmer over medium-high heat. Reduce the heat to medium-low and cook, covered, for 20 to 30 minutes, or until the potatoes are tender when pierced with a fork. Transfer the potatoes to a shallow bowl or plate and cool slightly.

Trim off the ends of the potatoes and slice crosswise into thirds. Sprinkle the remaining ½ teaspoon salt over the potatoes.

Arrange the potato slices on a serving platter. Spoon a dollop of sour cream on each slice, then sprinkle with the caviar. Serve immediately. **Serves 4 to 6.**

Roasted Eggplant and Red Pepper Salsa

Serve this richly flavored salsa as a dip with
blue corn tortilla chips or as a topping for grilled meats or poultry.

2 medium Japanese
  eggplants (about 1 pound)

2 large red bell peppers

1 teaspoon canola
  or vegetable oil

1 cup fresh cilantro leaves

2 garlic cloves

1 tablespoon peeled fresh ginger

2 tablespoons Asian sesame oil

2 teaspoons sugar

1 tablespoon Chinese hot
  chili oil

¼ cup black Chinese vinegar
  or balsamic vinegar

⅔ cup chopped scallions
  (white & tender green parts)

1 teaspoon salt

Preheat the oven to 400° F. Prick the eggplant several times with a fork. Rub the eggplants and bell peppers all over with the oil and place on an ungreased baking sheet. Bake for 20 to 25 minutes, or until tender. Place the peppers in a small paper bag and close tightly to allow to steam. Set the eggplant aside to cool slightly.

Meanwhile, in a food processor fitted with the metal blade, combine ½ cup of cilantro, the garlic, ginger, sesame oil, sugar, chili oil, and vinegar and process until pureed. Set aside.

Coarsely chop the eggplant. Peel, seed, and coarsely chop the peppers.

In a medium-size bowl, combine the eggplant, peppers, the remaining ½ cup of cilantro, the scallions, and the salt. Stir in the garlic-ginger puree. Let stand at room temperature for 1 hour to allow the flavors to blend. (The salsa can be refrigerated in a covered container for up to 2 days. Bring to room temperature before serving.) **Makes 3 cups.**

California Rolls

This type of sushi is an unusual case of a "Japanese" dish that was actually invented in California and is now established in Japan. Short-grain rice is used here because it holds together well; its high starch content causes it to be sticky when cooked. Wasabi, sometimes called Japanese horseradish because of its pungent bite, is available in powder and paste form in Asian and specialty food markets. If you use the paste, simply omit the 2 teaspoons water.

Sushi Rice:

2½ cups short-grain white rice

¼ cup rice vinegar

3 tablespoons sugar

1½ teaspoons salt

2½ cups water

2 tablespoons dry sherry

2 teaspoons black sesame seeds

1 tablespoon wasabi powder

2 teaspoons water

1 seedless cucumber

1 ripe avocado, preferably Haas

2 sheets toasted nori (seaweed)

⅓ pound lump crabmeat,
  picked over

2 tablespoons flying fish roe
  or salmon caviar

Prepare the rice: Put the rice in a colander and rinse under cold water, tossing with a spoon, until the water runs clear. Let drain for 30 minutes.

In a small saucepan, combine the vinegar, sugar, and salt and cook over medium heat, stirring frequently, for 1 minute, or until the sugar is dissolved. Remove the pan from the heat.

In a medium-size saucepan, combine the rice, water, and sherry. Cover and bring to a boil over high heat. Reduce the heat to medium and cook for 12 minutes. Remove the pan from the heat and let stand, covered, for 10 minutes, or until the rice is tender and

all the liquid is absorbed.

Spread the rice out in a nonreactive baking pan. Sprinkle the rice with the vinegar mixture while gently tossing with a stainless steel fork. Cover with a damp cloth and let stand at room temperature until ready to use. (The rolls should be assembled no more than 1 hour before serving.)

In a small skillet, toast the sesame seeds over medium heat, stirring frequently, for 1 minute, or until fragrant. Remove the pan from the heat.

In a small bowl, mix the wasabi with the water to form a paste.

Cut the cucumber lengthwise into 4 equal strips. Peel and pit the avocado and cut lengthwise into 16 equal strips.

Cut the sheets of nori in half crosswise. Lay 1 piece, shiny side down, with a long edge facing you, on a bamboo mat for rolling sushi or a sheet of waxed paper.

Moisten your hands with water, then spread about 1¼ cups of the rice over the nori, leaving a ½-inch border at the top. Brush ¼ teaspoon of the wasabi paste in a line down the center of the rice. Lay a cucumber slice on top of the wasabi. Cover the cucumber with one quarter of the crabmeat, sprinkle ½ teaspoon of the sesame seeds over the crab, and lay 4 slices of avocado on top. Starting with a long end and using the mat or paper as a guide, roll the nori up over the filling into a compact cylinder and set aside. Repeat with the remaining ingredients.

To serve, cut each roll into 6 pieces. Place cut side up on a platter and sprinkle the tops with the fish roe. Serve the remaining wasabi on the side. **Makes 24 pieces**.

Grilled Baguettes with Fresh Tomato Relish

The success of this simple appetizer depends on using
the best-quality ingredients ~ fresh crusty bread, extra-virgin olive oil, and
ripe tomatoes. It's a good dish to prepare in late summer, when farmers'
markets are bursting with countless varieties of juicy tomatoes.

Fresh Tomato Relish:

*2 medium ripe tomatoes, finely
chopped*

1 small garlic clove, minced

8 fresh basil leaves, shredded

*1 tablespoon extra-virgin
olive oil*

¼ teaspoon salt

¼ teaspoon black pepper

*2 tablespoons extra-virgin
olive oil*

1 small garlic clove, crushed

*16 slices French baguette, about
½ inch thick*

Prepare the relish: In a medium-size nonreactive bowl, gently toss together the tomatoes, garlic, basil, oil, salt, and pepper. Set aside.

Preheat the broiler. In a small skillet, heat the remaining oil over low heat. Add the crushed garlic, then remove the skillet from the heat and set aside.

Put the bread slices on an ungreased baking sheet. Broil 4 inches from the heat source on 1 side only for 1 to 2 minutes, or until golden brown. Remove from the broiler and brush the toasted sides with the garlic oil.

To serve, arrange the bread slices toasted side up on a serving platter and spoon the tomato relish over them. Serve immediately. **Serves 6 to 8.**

Caesar Salad

It is widely believed that this salad was created in Mexico by Caesar Cardini, an Italian chef who owned a restaurant in Tijuana, but it has become closely associated with California cuisine.

Garlic Croutons:

2 tablespoons olive oil

1 garlic clove, crushed

5 slices French bread, crusts
removed & cut into ½-inch cubes

Caesar Dressing:

1 garlic clove, chopped

6 anchovy fillets, drained

1 teaspoon Worcestershire sauce

1 large egg yolk

1 tablespoon fresh lemon juice

¼ teaspoon salt

¼ teaspoon black pepper

⅓ cup extra-virgin olive oil

2 small heads romaine lettuce,
separated into leaves

1 cup grated Parmesan cheese

Prepare the croutons: In a medium-size skillet, heat the oil over medium heat. Add the garlic and cook, stirring frequently, for 2 minutes, or until golden. Remove and discard the garlic. Add the bread cubes, tossing to coat with the oil, and cook, stirring frequently, for 4 minutes, or until golden. Remove to paper towels to drain.

Prepare the dressing: In a food processor fitted with the metal blade, combine all the dressing ingredients except the oil and process until well blended. With the motor running, gradually add oil through the feed tube in a thin steady stream until combined.

In a large bowl, toss together the lettuce, cheese, and croutons. Add the dressing, tossing to coat. Transfer the salad to individual serving plates. **Serves 4.**

Baby Spinach Salad with Curry Dressing

Almonds, apples, dried apricots, and tender spinach leaves combine
for a nutritious salad that strikes a balance of color, texture, and flavor. It makes
a great light lunch served with fresh, crusty sourdough bread.

Curry Dressing:

1 small garlic clove, minced

1 teaspoon curry powder

*1 teaspoon peeled minced
fresh ginger*

¾ teaspoon sugar

¼ teaspoon salt

¼ teaspoon black pepper

*1½ tablespoons white
wine vinegar*

*¼ cup dry California white wine
such as sauvignon blanc*

½ cup canola or vegetable oil

*2 medium tart apples such as
Granny Smith, peeled,
cored & cut into ½-inch pieces*

*¼ cup finely chopped
dried apricots*

*1 pound baby spinach leaves,
rinsed well*

½ cup sliced almonds, toasted

Prepare the dressing: In a food processor fitted with the metal blade, combine the garlic, curry powder, ginger, sugar, salt, pepper, vinegar, and wine and process until well blended. With the motor running, gradually add the oil through the feed tube in a thin steady stream until combined. Transfer the dressing to a medium-size bowl and stir in the apples and apricots. Let stand at room temperature for 1 hour to allow the flavors to blend.

Put the spinach leaves in a salad bowl. Add half the dressing, tossing to coat. Add the remaining dressing and toss to coat. Sprinkle with the toasted almonds and serve. **Serves 4 to 6.**

Goat Cheese Salad with Hazelnut Vinaigrette

California produces a variety of specialty cheeses, including many made from goat's milk. Also known as chèvre, goat cheese has a distinctly tart flavor. In this recipe, it is baked until very soft and meltingly creamy.

½ cup hazelnuts

6 ounces soft goat cheese

¼ pound mixed lettuces, preferably including baby red lettuce, escarole, arugula, radicchio & endive

Hazelnut Vinaigrette:

2 tablespoons extra-virgin olive oil

1 tablespoon hazelnut oil

1 tablespoon tarragon vinegar

Salt & black pepper

Preheat the oven to 400°F. Spread the hazelnuts on an ungreased baking sheet and toast for 10 to 12 minutes, or until the skins begin to flake. Transfer the nuts to a kitchen towel, fold the towel over them, and rub vigorously to remove the skins. Discard the skins. On a cutting board, coarsely chop the nuts, and set aside to cool.

Form the goat cheese into 6 rounds about 2 inches in diameter. Coat the rounds completely with the chopped hazelnuts and transfer to an ungreased baking sheet. Bake for 5 to 8 minutes, or until warmed through but not melted.

Tear the lettuce into bite-size pieces and transfer to a shallow medium-size bowl. Prepare the vinaigrette: In a small bowl, whisk together both oils and the vinegar. Season to taste with salt and pepper.

Toss the lettuces with the vinaigrette. Arrange the salad on individual serving plates. Using a metal spatula, transfer 1 warm goat cheese round to each salad. **Serves 6.**

Calamari and Three-Pepper Salad

The best calamari (squid) come from the Sea of Cortez, between
Baja California and the Mexican mainland. The secret to tender squid is not
to overcook it ~ a minute too long, and it will become rubbery.

Anchovy Dressing:

5 garlic cloves

1 small serrano chile pepper,
   stemmed & seeded

10 anchovy fillets, drained

½ cup fresh basil leaves

½ cup fresh parsley leaves

½ teaspoon salt

½ teaspoon black pepper

⅓ cup red wine vinegar

1 tablespoon fresh lemon juice

½ cup extra-virgin olive oil

Calamari Salad:

1 pound cleaned calamari

8 cups water

2 teaspoons salt

1 small green bell pepper,
   seeded & cut into thin strips

1 small red bell pepper,
   seeded & cut into thin strips

1 small yellow bell pepper,
   seeded & cut into thin strips

1 head frisée (curly escarole),
   torn into pieces

Prepare the dressing: In a food processor fitted with the metal blade, combine the garlic, chile pepper, anchovies, basil, and parsley and process until finely chopped. Add the salt, black pepper, vinegar, and lemon juice and process until combined. With the motor running, pour the olive oil through the feed tube in a thin steady stream until combined. Set aside.

Prepare the salad: Cut the calamari bodies into ½-inch rounds. Leave the tentacles whole. In a medium-size saucepan, bring the water and salt to a boil over high heat. Add the squid and cook for 30 seconds. Drain, rinse

under cold water, and drain again.

In a medium-size nonreactive bowl, combine the squid, bell peppers, and dressing and toss to coat. Cover with plastic wrap and chill for 4 hours, stirring occasionally, to allow the flavors to blend.

To serve, arrange the frisée on individual plates and spoon the salad on top. **Serves 6**.

Arugula Salad with
Dry Monterey Jack and Bacon

(picture p. 59)

This zesty salad with a hearty, robust taste is a snap to put together. Arugula, also called rocket, has slender dark green leaves and a peppery mustard flavor.

Lemon Dressing:

1 teaspoon grated lemon zest

1 tablespoon fresh lemon juice

½ teaspoon Dijon-style mustard

½ teaspoon sugar

1 small garlic clove, minced

¼ cup extra-virgin olive oil

Salt & black pepper

Arugula Salad:

4 thick slices applewood-smoked bacon or other smoked bacon, cut into 1-inch pieces

⅓ pound arugula, rinsed

1 cup grated dry Monterey Jack cheese

Prepare the dressing: In a small bowl, combine the lemon zest, lemon juice, mustard, sugar, and garlic until well blended. Gradually whisk in the olive oil in a thin steady stream until combined. Season to taste with salt and pepper. Set aside.

Prepare the salad: In a medium-size skillet, cook the bacon over medium heat, stirring frequently, for about 3 minutes, or until crisp. Remove to paper towels to drain.

In a medium-size bowl, toss the arugula with the dressing. Add the bacon and cheese and toss to combine. **Serves 6.**

Three-Tomato Salad with Two-Basil Dressing

This salad takes advantage of the explosion of tomato varieties
that now appear seasonally in specialty produce markets. The key here is to use
vine-ripened tomatoes at their peak of freshness. If you can't find
purple basil, use all sweet basil.

Three-Tomato Salad:

3 medium ripe red tomatoes

*12 ripe yellow pear tomatoes,
stemmed & cut in
half lengthwise*

*18 small ripe cherry tomatoes,
stemmed*

Two-Basil Dressing:

*1 medium ripe red tomato,
peeled, seeded & chopped*

12 fresh sweet basil leaves

12 fresh purple basil leaves

¼ cup chopped onion

1 teaspoon Dijon-style mustard

1 teaspoon sugar

2 tablespoons white wine vinegar

⅓ cup olive oil

Salt & black pepper

Prepare the salad: Cut the medium-size red tomatoes into quarters, then cut each quarter into 2 wedges. In a medium-size nonreactive bowl, combine all the tomatoes.

Prepare the dressing: In a food processor fitted with the metal blade, combine the tomato, 4 leaves of each type of basil, the onion, mustard, sugar, and vinegar and process until pureed. With the motor running, gradually add the oil through the feed tube in a thin steady stream until combined. Season to taste with salt and pepper.

Finely shred the remaining basil leaves. Pour the dressing over the tomatoes, tossing gently to coat. Add half the shredded basil and toss to combine. Sprinkle the remaining shredded basil over the top. **Serves 6 to 8.**

Thai Noodle Salad

Thai cuisine, with its emphasis on freshness and flavor,
has become enormously popular on the West Coast. Fresh cilantro,
basil, and mint are critical to the flavor of this dish.

Spicy Ginger Dressing:

3 garlic cloves, minced

One 1-inch piece ginger,
  peeled & minced

¼ cup fresh lime juice

1 tablespoon Thai or
  Vietnamese fish sauce

1 small jalapeño pepper,
  seeded & finely chopped

1 tablespoon sugar

½ teaspoon salt

¾ cup canola oil

Thai Salad:

8 ounces dried vermicelli

4 scallions, cut into thin strips
  (white & tender green parts)

1 small carrot, cut into
  thin strips

2 tablespoons chopped fresh basil

2 tablespoons chopped fresh
  cilantro

2 tablespoons chopped fresh mint

4 to 6 lettuce leaves

Prepare the dressing: In a food processor fitted with the metal blade, combine all the ingredients except the oil and process until blended. With the motor running, gradually add the oil through the feed tube in a thin steady stream until combined. Set aside.

Prepare the salad: Bring a large saucepan of salted water to a boil over high heat.

Cook the vermicelli in the boiling water for 8 to 10 minutes, or until al dente; drain well.

In a medium-size bowl, combine the vermicelli, scallions, carrot, basil, cilantro, and mint. Add the dressing and toss to coat. To serve, arrange the lettuce leaves on serving plates, and spoon the salad on top. **Serves 4 to 6.**

Chinese Chicken Salad

This strictly Chinese-American creation is a big favorite with Californians. Rice-flour noodles are thin translucent strands that expand into a crunchy tangle when deep-fried. They are available in Asian markets and some supermarkets.

Chicken Salad:

1 tablespoon soy sauce

1 tablespoon hoisin sauce

1 tablespoon dry sherry

3 boneless & skinless chicken breast halves (about 1¼ pounds)

2 cups plus 2 tablespoons vegetable oil

1 small head iceberg lettuce, shredded

5 scallions, chopped (white & tender green parts)

1 cup fresh cilantro leaves

1 cup roasted salted peanuts, coarsely chopped (optional)

4 ounces dried rice-flour noodles

Sesame Dressing:

⅓ cup fresh lemon juice

3 tablespoons hoisin sauce

1 teaspoon Asian sesame oil

Prepare the salad: In a shallow bowl, combine the soy sauce, hoisin sauce, and sherry. Add the chicken, turning to coat. Cover with plastic wrap and marinate at room temperature, turning once, for 30 minutes.

In a medium-size skillet, heat 2 tablespoons of vegetable oil over medium-high heat. Add the chicken and cook for 8 minutes, turning once, or until browned on both sides.

Transfer the chicken to a plate and let cool.

In a medium-size bowl, toss together the lettuce, scallions, cilantro, and peanuts if desired. Set aside.

In a deep medium-size skillet, heat the remaining 2 cups oil over medium-high heat to 350°F, or until hot but not smoking. Break off a handful of the rice noodles and add them to the hot oil; they will immediately

puff up. Using tongs, turn the noodles and cook a few seconds, or until they cease to expand. Remove to paper towels to drain. Cook the remaining noodles in batches.

Cut the chicken crosswise into thin strips. Add the chicken, with any accumulated juices, to the lettuce and toss to combine.

Prepare the dressing: In a small bowl, whisk together the lemon juice, hoisin sauce, and sesame oil. Pour the dressing over the salad and toss to coat.

To serve, arrange the noodles on individual serving plates and spoon the chicken salad over them. **Serves 6**.

Saffron-Scented Mussel Soup

On the California coast, mussel season traditionally opens
on the first of November. However, aquaculture makes these bivalves
available year-round, so you don't really have to wait to enjoy them.
This soup makes a delicious first course for dinner, or it can stand alone
as a light lunch. Select mussels about 1½ to 2 inches long; larger
ones have less flavor and tend to be tougher.

1 cup dry California white wine
such as sauvignon blanc

1 cup water

20 fresh mussels (about 1
pound), scrubbed & debearded

1 tablespoon unsalted butter

1 medium onion, finely chopped

¼ teaspoon saffron threads

½ cup heavy cream

1 cup fresh or frozen
corn kernels, thawed if frozen

1 tomato, peeled, seeded
& cut into ¼-inch pieces

Salt & black pepper

In a large saucepan, bring the wine and water to a boil over high heat. Add the mussels and cook, covered, for 5 minutes, or just until the shells open. Using a slotted spoon, transfer the mussels to a medium-size bowl, shaking any liquid back into the pan. Discard any mussels that do not open.

Strain the cooking liquid through a cheesecloth-lined fine sieve set over a small bowl to remove any grit. Set aside.

When the mussels are cool enough to handle, remove and discard the shells. Strain any liquid remaining in the mussel bowl through the cheesecloth-lined sieve into the cooking liquid.

In a medium-size saucepan, melt the butter over medium heat. Add the onion and cook, stirring frequently, for 5 minutes, or until it begins to soften.

Rub the saffron threads between your

Lone cypress, Carmel

fingers to crumble, then add to the onion. Add the reserved cooking liquid and the cream and cook, stirring frequently, for 2 minutes. Add the corn and cook, stirring occasionally, for 2 minutes. Add the tomato and cook for 1 minute. Season to taste with salt and pepper.

To serve, divide the mussels among 4 soup bowls and ladle the hot soup over them. **Serves 4**.

North Beach Cioppino

Cioppino is a seafood stew that has been attributed to both the Portuguese and Italian fishermen who fished the northern California coast for over a century.

1 cooked Dungeness crab
(about 1½ to 2 pounds)

2 tablespoons olive oil

1 large onion, chopped

3 garlic cloves, minced

1 large green bell pepper,
seeded & chopped

2½ cups canned tomatoes,
coarsley chopped & drained

2 tablespoons tomato paste

¼ teaspoon dried basil

¼ teaspoon dried oregano

¼ teaspoon dried thyme

¼ cup chopped fresh parsley

2 cups dry California red wine
such as cabernet sauvignon

1 teaspoon salt

½ teaspoon black pepper

1 pound rock cod or haddock,
cut into 2-inch pieces

1 dozen littleneck or cherrystone
clams, in their shells

1 dozen large shrimp, in
their shells

Pull the legs from the crab and gently crack them. Working over a shallow bowl to collect the juices, remove the crab body from the shell and clean off the gills and fibrous gray matter attached to it; discard the shell. Scrape the yellow crab butter from the body and add to the juices. Cut the body into quarters and set aside.

In a Dutch oven, heat the oil over medium-high heat. Add the onion, garlic, and bell pepper and cook, stirring frequently, for 5 minutes, or until the vegetables begin to soften. Add the tomatoes, breaking them up with a spoon, and cook, stirring frequently, for 5 minutes. Stir in the tomato paste, crab juices, herbs, wine, salt, and black pepper and

cook over medium heat, stirring occasionally, for 20 minutes.

Add the cod and clams and cook, stirring occasionally, for 5 minutes. Add the shrimp and cook, covered, for 5 minutes. Add the crab and cook, covered, for 5 minutes more, or until the clams have opened and the shrimp have turned pink and opaque.

Ladle the soup into individual serving bowls and serve immediately. **Serves 6 to 8.**

Cream of Corn Soup with Chile Chipotle

Once again, California chefs have raided the Mexican kitchen for
a delicious soup. Chiles chipotle are jalapeño peppers that have been dried by
smoking over a wood fire. They are sold loose-packed or canned in adobo
(or adobado) sauce, a pungent paste made from chiles, herbs, and vinegar, available
in Latin American markets and some large supermarkets.

2 tablespoons unsalted butter

1 medium onion, chopped

*1 canned chile chipotle in
    adobo sauce*

*5 cups fresh or frozen
    corn kernels, thawed if frozen*

2 cups milk

Salt

3 tablespoons sour cream

*Sprigs of fresh cilantro,
    for garnish (optional)*

In a medium-size saucepan, melt the butter over medium heat. Add the onion and cook, stirring frequently, for 5 minutes, or until softened. Add the chile, breaking it up with a spoon. Add the corn and milk. Reduce the heat to low and cook, stirring occasionally, for 10 minutes, or until the corn is very tender; do not boil.

Transfer the soup to a blender or a food processor fitted with the metal blade and process until pureed. Strain through a sieve set over a medium-size bowl. Return the soup to another saucepan and warm over low heat. Season to taste with salt.

Meanwhile, in a small bowl, combine the sour cream and 1 teaspoon of the canned adobo sauce.

To serve, ladle the hot soup into 4 bowls and put a spoonful of the sour cream mixture on top of each serving. Garnish with cilantro, if desired. **Serves 4.**

Garlic Mashed Potatoes

This is a simply heavenly version of the most traditional American potato dish. For best results, use Yellow Finn potatoes, which are grown in the Pacific Northwest and are available in specialty produce markets. This recipe brings out the creamy texture and buttery flavor of the potatoes.

2½ pounds medium Yellow Finn or Idaho potatoes, peeled & quartered

2 large garlic heads, cloves separated & peeled

¼ cup (½ stick) unsalted butter, softened

½ cup half-and-half, warmed

Salt & white pepper

Bring a large saucepan of salted water to a boil over high heat. Add the potatoes and garlic, reduce the heat to medium-high, and boil gently, uncovered, for about 20 minutes, or until the potatoes and garlic are tender. Drain well; set aside the cooking liquid.

Transfer the potatoes and garlic to a large bowl. Add the butter and coarsely mash the potatoes and garlic with a potato masher or fork. Make a well in the center of the potatoes and pour in the warm half-and-half. Using a hand-held electric mixer, beat the mixture just until light and creamy. If necessary, add some of the reserved cooking liquid to achieve a smooth, fluffy texture. Season to taste with salt and pepper. Serve immediately. **Serves 6**.

Roasted Whole Garlic

Gilroy, California, is known as the garlic capital of the world,
so it's no surprise that Californians consume a lot of the pungent little cloves.
This is a dish you can enjoy twice: first while it is cooking and the delicious
smell of roasting garlic fills the kitchen, and then when you eat it. Roasted
garlic is a creamy delight with a deep, sweet, mild flavor.

*4 large garlic heads, with
plump cloves*

1 tablespoon olive oil

1 teaspoon salt

½ cup dry white wine

*Several sprigs of fresh rosemary,
thyme, or marjoram*

1 bay leaf

French bread, sliced

Preheat the oven to 400°F.

Slice ½ inch off the top of each head of garlic. Put the garlic heads in a small ovenproof pan that holds them snugly. Sprinkle with the olive oil and toss to coat. Set the heads stem ends down and sprinkle with the salt. Pour the wine into the pan and nestle the rosemary and bay leaf around the garlic.

Cover the pan tightly with foil. Bake for 1 hour. Remove the foil and continue baking for 15 minutes, or until the garlic is very tender.

Arrange the heads on a serving plate. To eat, remove a clove of garlic from the cluster with a small knife, discard the papery skins, and squeeze or spread on a slice of bread. **Serves 8 to 10**.

Couscous with Fruited Vegetable Sauce

(picture p. 67)

The sauce for this healthful vegetarian dish makes use of dates and apricots, both major California crops. Couscous (dried semolina) is sold in Middle Eastern markets, health food stores, and some supermarkets.

Fruited Vegetable Sauce:

2 tablespoons olive oil

1 medium onion, chopped

2 garlic cloves, minced

½ teaspoon cinnamon

Salt

½ teaspoon ground cumin

¼ teaspoon allspice

1 cup dry California white wine such as sauvignon blanc

½ cup dried apricots, cut into quarters

½ cup dates, pitted & cut in half lengthwise

1 small carrot, peeled & cut into ½-inch slices

1 small zucchini, cut into ½-inch slices

2 cups cooked garbanzo beans (chick-peas)

1 cup chopped fresh cilantro leaves

Couscous:

1½ cups couscous

2½ cups water

1 teaspoon salt

⅛ teaspoon turmeric

Fresh sage, for garnish (optional)

Prepare the sauce: In a large skillet, heat the oil over medium heat. Add the onion and cook, stirring frequently, for 5 minutes, or until softened. Add the garlic and cook, stirring frequently, for 1 minute. Add the cinna- mon, 1 teaspoon of salt, the cumin, and the allspice. Cook, stirring frequently, for 2 minutes, or until the spices are fragrant and begin to stick to the bottom of the skillet. Stir in the wine, and add the apricots, dates,

The San Francisco skyline

carrot, zucchini, garbanzo beans, and cilantro. Bring to a boil over high heat. Reduce the heat to low and cook, covered, stirring occasionally, for 20 minutes, or until the fruits and vegetables are softened and most of the liquid is absorbed. Season to taste with salt and remove from the heat.

Meanwhile, prepare the couscous: In a medium-size saucepan, combine the water, salt, and turmeric and bring to a boil over high heat. Add the couscous and stir well. Remove the pan from the heat, cover, and let stand for 15 minutes.

To serve, fluff the couscous with a fork, spread it on a serving platter, and spoon the sauce over it. Garnish with fresh sage, if desired. **Serves 4 to 6.**

Orange-Glazed Asparagus and Shiitake Mushrooms

Shiitake mushrooms, which have been cultivated in Japan for at least 1,500 years, are very popular in California. They are valued for their large, meaty brown caps; the tough stems are usually discarded. Here the rich, smoky flavor of the mushroom is accented by a tangy orange glaze and delicate asparagus.

1 pound thin asparagus spears

1 tablespoon butter

4 ounces fresh shiitake mushrooms, stemmed & thinly sliced

⅓ cup fresh orange juice

½ teaspoon salt

Pinch of cayenne

2 teaspoons grated orange zest

Black pepper

Snap off and discard the tough ends of the asparagus. Cut each spear diagonally into 3 pieces.

In a medium-size nonreactive skillet, melt the butter over medium heat. Add the asparagus and cook, stirring frequently, for 4 minutes, or until bright green but still firm. Add the mushrooms and cook, stirring frequently, for 2 to 3 minutes, or until they begin to soften.

Stir in the orange juice, salt, and cayenne. Cook, covered, for 3 minutes, or until the asparagus is tender. (If there is a lot of liquid remaining in the skillet, increase the heat to medium-high and cook, uncovered, stirring frequently, until most of it has evaporated.)

To serve, transfer the vegetables to a serving platter. Sprinkle with the orange zest and season to taste with pepper. **Serves 4.**

Steamed Artichokes with Basil Aïoli

Castroville, California, is the self-proclaimed artichoke capital of the world. Here you can find these globe-shaped vegetables in an assortment of sizes ~ from the baby variety, which measures 2 inches or less in diameter, to those that weigh as much as 2 pounds. Steaming is a particularly good way to prepare artichokes because it seals in both flavor and nutrients. Served with a garlicky basil mayonnaise, this dish can be enjoyed warm or chilled and is perfect for informal summer entertaining.

6 medium to large
  artichokes, about
  10 ounces each

1 lemon, sliced

1 tablespoon olive oil

1 teaspoon salt

Basil Aïoli:

1 cup fresh basil leaves

6 garlic cloves

1 large egg

1½ teaspoons fresh lemon juice

1 cup mild extra-virgin olive oil

Fresh chives, for garnish (optional)

Using a sharp knife, cut off the stems of the artichokes flush with the bottoms and pull off the leaves at the base. Trim off the sharp leaf tips with kitchen scissors. Rub the freshly cut parts with a lemon slice to prevent discoloration.

Fill a large saucepan or Dutch oven with 2 inches of water. Add the remaining lemon slices, oil, and salt. Set the artichokes upright in the pan on a steamer. Steam over medium heat, covered, for 35 to 45 minutes, or until the leaves pull off easily.

Meanwhile, prepare the aïoli: In a food processor fitted with the metal blade, combine the basil, garlic, egg, and lemon juice and process until pureed. With the motor running, gradually add the oil through the feed tube in a thin steady stream until combined.

Transfer to a small bowl and set aside.

Drain the artichokes upside down in a colander. When cool enough to handle, carefully spread the outer leaves of each artichoke to expose the choke. Remove and discard the small leaves in the center and scrape out the fuzzy choke with a spoon.

To serve, place the artichokes on individual serving plates. Fill the artichoke centers with some of the aïoli, for dipping the leaves. Garnish the aïoli with the chives, if desired. Pass any remaining aïoli at the table. **Serves 6.**

Black Bean Chili

When you want something different, try this vegetarian chili.
Ancho and guajillo chiles add a rich, intense flavor to the dish. Serve with warm
corn or flour tortillas on the side, or wrap in tortillas for quick burritos.

2 cups dried black beans,
 picked over & rinsed

1 tablespoon plus
 1 teaspoon cumin seeds

1 bay leaf

2 dried ancho chiles,
 stemmed & seeded

2 dried guajillo chiles,
 stemmed & seeded

1 teaspoon coriander seeds

1 medium onion, quartered

3 garlic cloves, minced

1 canned chile chipotle
 in adobo sauce

5 large ripe tomatoes, peeled,
 seeded & chopped, or 5 cups
 canned tomatoes, chopped

1 teaspoon salt, or to taste

Toppings:

1 medium onion,
 finely chopped

5 to 6 scallions, finely chopped
 (white & tender green parts)

½ cup chopped fresh cilantro
 leaves

1 cup shredded Monterey
 Jack cheese

In a medium-size saucepan, combine the beans with enough cold water to cover by 2 inches. Add 1 tablespoon of the cumin seeds and the bay leaf and bring to a boil over high heat. Reduce the heat to low and simmer uncovered, for 1 hour.

Meanwhile, put the dried chiles in a small saucepan and add enough cold water to cover. Bring to a boil over high heat. Remove the pan from the heat, cover, and let stand for 15 minutes. Drain, reserving 1 cup of cooking liquid.

Grand Central Market, Los Angeles

In a small dry skillet, combine the remaining 1 teaspoon cumin seeds and the coriander seeds. Toast over medium heat, stirring frequently, for 1 to 2 minutes, or until fragrant. Remove the pan from the heat.

In a food processor fitted with the metal blade, combine the toasted seeds, drained chiles, onion, garlic, chile chipotle, and 2½ cups of the tomatoes and process until pureed. Pour the mixture into a large skillet and cook over medium heat, stirring frequently, for 5 minutes, or until the puree thickens slightly. Set aside.

After the beans have cooked for 1 hour, stir in the puree. Add the reserved cooking liquid from the dried chiles to the skillet, stirring to scrape up any bits from the bottom of the pan, and add this mixture to the beans.

Cook the beans, partially covered, stirring occasionally, for 1 hour more, or until just tender. Add the remaining tomatoes with their juice and the salt and cook, stirring occasionally, for 20 to 30 minutes. Discard the bay leaf.

To serve, put each topping into a small bowl. Spoon the chili into individual bowls and serve with the toppings. **Serves 6 to 8.**

Warm New Potato Salad

Red-skinned new potatoes are the best choice for this salad
because they keep their shape and texture when cooked and quartered. With
its roasted garlic flavoring, this salad makes a delicious accompaniment
to Medallions of Pork with Gravenstein Apple Cider Sauce (p. 58) or Mesquite-
Grilled Duck with Cranberry Salsa (p. 63).

10 garlic cloves

2 pounds medium
  red-skinned new potatoes

1 tablespoon salt

2 tablespoons olive oil

1 tablespoon balsamic vinegar

1 teaspoon minced fresh parsley

1 teaspoon fresh marjoram

1 teaspoon fresh rosemary leaves,
  crumbled

1 teaspoon fresh thyme

½ teaspoon black pepper

Preheat the oven to 400°F. Wrap the garlic in aluminum foil and bake for 30 minutes, or until soft. Set aside.

Meanwhile, put the potatoes into a large saucepan with enough water to cover by 3 inches. Add 2 teaspoons of the salt and bring to a boil over high heat. Reduce the heat to medium and cook, uncovered, for 15 minutes, or until just tender when pierced with a fork. Drain well. When cool enough to handle, cut the potatoes into quarters, transfer to a baking pan large enough to hold them in a single layer, and set aside.

In a food processor fitted with the metal blade, combine the roasted garlic, oil, vinegar, and the remaining 1 teaspoon salt and process until pureed. Pour the garlic mixture over the potatoes, tossing to coat.

Bake for 15 minutes. Sprinkle with the herbs and pepper, tossing to coat. Bake for another 5 to 10 minutes, or until the potatoes begin to turn golden. Serve warm. **Serves 6.**

Pan-Roasted Coriander Sea Bass

This recipe uses both the seed and leaves of the coriander plant
(the leaves are known as cilantro) for an interesting blend of flavors and textures.
If sea bass is unavailable, substitute grouper or cod.

Cilantro Sauce:

*1 cup packed fresh cilantro
leaves & stems*

1 cup packed butter lettuce leaves

⅓ cup heavy cream

*¼ cup dry California white wine
such as chardonnay*

½ teaspoon salt

¼ teaspoon white pepper

2 tablespoons coriander seeds

*4 sea bass fillets, 5 to 6 ounces
each, cut 1 inch thick*

2 teaspoons olive oil

Prepare the sauce: In a food processor fitted with the metal blade, combine the cilantro, lettuce, cream, wine, salt, and pepper and process until pureed. Strain the sauce through a fine sieve set over a medium-size saucepan.

Cook the sauce over medium heat, stirring frequently, for 3 minutes. Remove the pan from the heat and season to taste with salt and pepper. Keep warm.

Using a mortar and pestle or the side of a cleaver, crush the coriander seeds. Press ½ tablespoon of the crushed seeds into 1 side of each fillet. In a large nonstick skillet, heat the oil over medium-high heat. Add the fillets seed side down, reduce the heat to medium, and cook, covered, for 5 minutes. Turn the fish and cook, uncovered, for 2 minutes, then turn again and cook for another 2 minutes.

Divide the sauce among 4 individual serving plates and place a fish fillet, seed side up, on each plate. **Serves 4.**

Pan-Seared Ahi Tuna with Caramelized Vegetables

Ahi tuna has become very popular on the West Coast. It has a rich,
deep, meaty flavor but is also compatible with a health-conscious diet. The sauce
borrows the sweet-and-sour concept that characterizes so many Asian dishes.

Caramelized Vegetables:

1 tablespoon olive oil

1 tablespoon unsalted butter

¼ cup dark raisins

¼ cup pine nuts

*2 medium onions, cut into
¼-inch slices*

*2 medium red bell peppers, seeded
& cut into ½-inch pieces*

½ teaspoon salt

2 tablespoons red wine vinegar

1 tablespoon sugar

1 tablespoon olive oil

1 teaspoon salt

*6 ahi tuna steaks, 5 to 6 ounces
each, about ½ inch thick*

Prepare the vegetables: In a medium-size skillet, heat the oil and butter over medium heat. Add the raisins and pine nuts and cook, stirring frequently, for 2 minutes, or until the raisins are plumped and the nuts are golden. Remove with a slotted spoon to a plate and set aside.

Add the onions to the skillet and cook over medium-low heat, stirring frequently, for 10 minutes, or until softened. Add the peppers and salt and cook, stirring occasionally, for 10 minutes, or until the peppers are softened. Stir in the vinegar and sugar and cook, stirring occasionally, for 5 minutes. Return the raisins and pine nuts to the skillet and cook over low heat, stirring occasionally, for 5 to 10 minutes, or until the vegetable are caramelized. Remove the skillet from the heat and keep warm.

In a large heavy skillet, heat the oil over high heat. When hot, sprinkle the skillet with

the salt and add the tuna steaks. Cook for 6 minutes, turning once, or until the fish is just opaque but still pink in the center. (Cook in batches if necessary.)

To serve, place the tuna steaks on individual serving plates and spoon the caramelized vegetables on top. **Serves 6**.

West Coast Crab and Shark Cakes with Lime-Cilantro Sauce

These Pacific Rim seafood cakes are a cross between the classic Maryland version and the denser fish cakes popular in Asia. The mayonnaise-style sauce uses both lime zest and lime juice, which lend texture and an interesting, slightly bitter flavor. If you can't find shark, substitute red snapper or cod fillets.

Lime-Cilantro Sauce:

1 large egg

1 cup fresh cilantro leaves

1 teaspoon Dijon-style mustard

3 scallions, chopped
   (white & tender green parts)

1 teaspoon peeled minced
   fresh ginger

1½ tablespoons fresh lime juice

1 teaspoon grated lime zest

1 cup canola oil

Crab & Shark Cakes:

½ pound shark, cut into
   1-inch pieces

1 large egg

½ teaspoon salt

½ pound lump crabmeat, picked over

1 cup dry bread crumbs

3 tablespoons canola or
   vegetable oil

6 cups shredded mixed lettuces

Lime wedges, for garnish (optional)

Prepare the sauce: In a food processor fitted with the metal blade, combine all the sauce ingredients except the oil and process until finely chopped. With the motor running, gradually add the oil through the feed tube in a thin steady stream and process until the sauce is the consistency of mayonnaise. Transfer to a small bowl and set aside.

Prepare the cakes: In a food processor fitted with the metal blade, combine the shark, egg, salt, and ½ cup of the lime-cilantro sauce, and process by pulsing on and off to form a paste.

Transfer the shark mixture to a medium-size bowl. Using a fork, stir in the crabmeat and ⅓ cup of the bread crumbs until blended.

Using about ¼ cup of the seafood mixture for each cake, form into 2-inch-wide discs. (You should have 8 cakes.) Spread the remaining bread crumbs on a plate. Coat the cakes completely with the bread crumbs.

Preheat the oven to 200°F. In a large skillet, heat the oil over medium-high heat.

Cook the cakes, in batches, for about 3 minutes on each side, or until golden brown and cooked through. Remove each batch to paper towels to drain and keep warm in the oven while you cook the remaining cakes.

To serve, arrange the lettuce on 4 individual serving plates. Place 2 cakes on each and drizzle with the remaining sauce. Garnish with lime wedges, if desired. **Serves 4**.

Salmon Fillet with Papaya-Avocado Salsa

The lush, tropical flavors of papaya and avocado match
the richness of salmon in this exotic dish. It can be served either warm or cold.

Papaya-Avocado Salsa:

*1 medium ripe papaya,
peeled, seeded & cut into
½-inch pieces*

*1 large ripe Haas avocado,
peeled, seeded & cut into
½-inch pieces*

6 tablespoons fresh lime juice

*2 serrano chile peppers,
seeded & finely chopped*

½ cup fresh cilantro leaves

*5 scallions, finely chopped
(white & tender green parts)*

*1 medium red bell pepper,
seeded & chopped*

Salt

1 salmon fillet, about 2 pounds

Salt

1 teaspoon olive oil

Papaya slices, for garnish (optional)

Avocado slices, for garnish (optional)

Prepare the salsa: In a medium-size nonreactive bowl, combine the papaya and avocado. Add the lime juice and toss gently to coat. Add the chiles, cilantro, scallions, and bell pepper and toss gently. Season to taste with salt. Set aside.

Using needle-nose pliers, remove any bones remaining in the salmon. Cut the salmon crosswise into 12 slices. Lightly sprinkle with salt on both sides.

In a large nonstick skillet, heat the oil over high heat. Add the salmon slices and cook over medium-high heat for 30 seconds on each side, or until just cooked through. (Cook in batches if necessary.)

To serve, arrange the salmon slices on individual serving plates, then garnish with slices of papaya and avocado, if desired. Serve the salsa on the side. **Serves 4 to 6.**

Orange Prawns with Mustard Greens

The sauce for this dish is flavored with two Asian ingredients, sesame oil and star anise, a star-shaped brown pod with a slightly bitter licorice flavor. Both are available in Asian markets.

40 prawns or large shrimp
  (about 2 pounds)

2 tablespoons grated orange zest

⅔ cup fresh orange juice

2 star anise

1 jalapeño pepper,
  seeded & finely chopped

1 teaspoon Asian sesame oil

Salt

3 large bunches mustard greens
  (about 1 pound), rinsed
  & coarsely chopped

¼ cup (½ stick) unsalted butter

3 garlic cloves, crushed

1 cup dry California white wine
  such as sauvignon blanc

1 cup water

Toasted black sesame seeds,
  for garnish (optional)

Peel and devein the prawns, reserving the shells.

In a medium-size nonreactive bowl, combine the prawns, 1 tablespoon of orange zest and the orange juice, star anise, jalapeño, sesame oil, and ½ teaspoon salt. Set aside at room temperature.

Place the mustard greens in a Dutch oven, and cook, covered, over medium heat for 5 minutes, or until wilted. (The water that clings to the leaves will steam and wilt them.)

Keep warm.

In a large skillet, melt the butter over medium heat. Add the garlic and cook, stirring frequently, for 1 minute, or until fragrant. Add the reserved prawn shells and cook, stirring frequently, for 5 minutes. Add the wine and water, increase the heat to medium-high, and cook, stirring occasionally, for 5 minutes.

Strain the mixture through a fine sieve set over a medium-size bowl, pressing on the

shells to extract all the liquid. Discard the shells and garlic, and return the sauce to the clean skillet. Cook over high heat, stirring constantly, for about 5 minutes, or until the sauce has thickened and begins to turn a light amber color.

Add the prawns with the marinade and cook, stirring frequently, for 3 to 5 minutes, or until the prawns have turned pink and are opaque. Season to taste with salt. Remove the skillet from the heat. Discard the star anise and cover to keep warm.

Spread the greens on a serving platter, making a well in the center. Spoon the prawns with the sauce into the well. Sprinkle with the remaining orange zest and the black sesame seeds, if desired, and serve immediately. **Serves 6 to 8.**

Medallions of Pork
with Gravenstein Apple Cider Sauce

The Gravenstein apple is an old variety that has recently
been resurrected by specialty growers in California and Washington State.
The apples are crisp, firm, and juicy with excellent flavor. If you can't find
Gravensteins, use a tart apple such as Granny Smith instead.

Apple Cider Sauce:

½ cup apple cider or apple juice

½ cup heavy cream

1 tablespoon apple cider vinegar

1 tablespoon Dijon-style seeded
  mustard

2 shallots, finely chopped

3 small sweet pickles (gherkins),
  thinly sliced crosswise

3 medium apples, peeled, cored
  & cut into ½-inch pieces

¼ teaspoon salt

¼ teaspoon black pepper

Medallions of Pork:

1 teaspoon butter

1 teaspoon olive oil

1½ pounds pork tenderloin, cut
  crosswise into ¾-inch slices

½ teaspoon salt

Prepare the sauce: In a medium-size non-reactive bowl, combine all the sauce ingredients and mix well. Set aside.

Prepare the pork: In a large skillet, heat the butter and oil over medium heat. Add the pork and sprinkle with the salt. Cook for 4 minutes on each side, or until the pork is almost cooked through and just barely pink in the center. (Cook in batches if necessary.) Transfer the pork slices to a plate.

Add the sauce to the skillet and cook, over medium-high heat stirring frequently, for

Medallions of Pork with Gravenstein Apple Cider Sauce
& Arugula Salad with Dry Monterey Jack and Bacon, page 26

8 to 10 minutes, or until the sauce has thickened and the apples are slightly softened. Return the pork to the skillet, reduce the heat to medium-low, and cook, stirring occasionally, for 5 minutes, or until the pork is just cooked through. Transfer the pork with the sauce to a serving platter. **Serves 4.**

Pot-Roasted Chicken with Sun-Dried Tomatoes and Garlic

Don't let the two heads of garlic frighten you away from this recipe: When roasted, the garlic becomes sweet and mild. For the best results, use a free-range chicken; it costs a bit more but is well worth it for the added flavor.

2 cups water

12 sun-dried tomatoes
(not packed in oil)

1 teaspoon minced fresh sage

1 teaspoon fresh rosemary
leaves, crumbled

½ teaspoon black pepper

One 3- to 3½-pound chicken

1 teaspoon salt

2 teaspoons olive oil

2 garlic heads, cloves
separated & peeled

In a small saucepan, combine the water and tomatoes and bring to a boil over high heat. Boil for 5 minutes. Drain the tomatoes, reserving the liquid, and set aside. Return the tomato liquid to the pan and boil for about 10 minutes, or until reduced to ¼ cup. Set aside.

Finely chop the tomatoes. In a small bowl, combine the tomatoes, sage, rosemary, and pepper.

Using your fingers, gently lift the chicken skin away from the flesh of the breasts and legs; try not to tear the skin. Stuff the tomato mixture under the loosened skin. Sprinkle the chicken cavity with salt. Tie the legs together using kitchen string.

In a large heavy nonstick saucepan or Dutch oven, heat the oil over medium-high heat. Add the chicken, breast side down. Scatter the garlic cloves over and around the chicken. Reduce the heat to medium-low and cook, covered, for 20 minutes.

Turn the chicken over and cook, covered, for 30 minutes more, or until the chicken

registers 165°F on a meat thermometer and the juices run clear when the thigh is pierced with a knife. Remove the chicken to a serving platter.

Add the reserved tomato water to the pan and cook, stirring constantly, over high heat for 2 minutes, or until thick and slightly syrupy. Spoon the sauce and garlic cloves over the chicken. **Serves 4.**

Pan-Fried Steaks in Red Wine Sauce

Cattle ranches have long been a large part of California's landscape and still are today. In fact, the beef industry is the second largest agriculture business in the state. Lean boneless strip steaks (also called club steaks) are used here, but cuts such as filet mignon can be substituted. Serve this dish with roasted new potatoes and a salad of mixed greens.

6 boneless strip steaks, 4 to 6 ounces each

2 teaspoons coarsely ground black pepper

1 teaspoon salt

1 cup dry California red wine such as cabernet sauvignon or zinfandel

⅓ cup heavy cream

Sprinkle the steaks on both sides with the pepper.

Heat a large heavy skillet over high heat. Sprinkle the pan with the salt. Add the steaks and cook over medium-high heat for about 4 minutes on each side, or until well browned. (Cook in batches if necessary.) Remove the steaks to a plate.

Add the wine to the skillet, stirring to scrape up any browned bits from the bottom of the pan. Cook, stirring occasionally, for about 4 minutes, or until the wine is reduced to about 3 tablespoons. Stir in the cream. Cook, stirring frequently, for 3 minutes, or until thickened.

Return the meat with any accumulated juices to the skillet. Spoon the sauce over the steaks and cook, uncovered, for 1 to 2 minutes for medium-rare, 2 to 3 minutes for medium.

Transfer the steaks to a serving platter. Spoon the sauce over the steaks and serve immediately. **Serves 6.**

Mesquite-Grilled Duck with Cranberry Salsa

Some of the best domestic ducks come from the area
around Petaluma, California, the largest duck-producing region west of
the Mississippi. A large kettle-type grill with a tight-fitting lid is best for this
dish because it works like a convection oven; the duck cooks evenly and
thoroughly without having to be turned. Fresh duck is available in specialty
markets, and frozen duck is sold in most supermarkets.

Mesquite-Grilled Duck:

One 4- to 5-pound fresh or
  frozen duck, thawed if frozen

2 teaspoons paprika

1 teaspoon garlic powder

½ teaspoon salt

¼ teaspoon ground coriander

¼ teaspoon black pepper

Pinch of cayenne

Pinch of cumin

5 pounds mesquite chips

Cranberry Salsa:

1 (12-ounce) bag fresh
  or frozen cranberries,
  thawed if frozen

½ cup sugar

⅓ cup fresh lime juice

2 large garlic cloves, minced

½ cup minced fresh
  cilantro leaves

1 small jalapeño pepper, seeded
  & finely chopped

3 scallions, finely chopped
  (white & tender green parts)

Salt

Prepare the duck: Rinse the duck and pat dry with paper towels. Pierce the skin all over with a fork or wooden skewer to allow the excess fat to drain off as the duck cooks; be careful not to puncture the flesh.

In a small bowl, combine the paprika, garlic powder, salt, coriander, black pepper, cayenne, and cumin. Rub this mixture all over

the duck, inside and out.

Prepare a grill fire, using the mesquite chips. Keep the bottom vents open and unobstructed by ash.

When the mesquite is burning white, divide it into 2 parts and place them on either side of the grill. Put a 9-by-13-inch heatproof pan between the 2 piles to catch the duck drippings. Place the grill rack over the mesquite chips and put the duck in the center of the rack. Close the lid, leaving its vents open. Cook for about 1 hour, or until the duck registers 160°F on a meat thermometer and the juices run clear when the thigh is pierced with a knife.

Meanwhile, prepare the salsa: In a medium-size saucepan, cover the cranberries with cold water. Bring to a boil over high heat and boil for 2 minutes, or until the cranberries start to pop. Drain well.

In a medium-size nonreactive bowl, combine the sugar and lime juice. Add the cranberries and gently stir in the garlic cloves, cilantro, jalapeño, and scallions. Season to taste with salt. Set aside at room temperature for 30 minutes to allow the flavors to blend.

Transfer the duck to a serving platter and let stand for 5 minutes. Carve and serve with the salsa on the side. **Serves 4**.

Grilled Leg of Lamb with Garlic and Mint Aïoli

This versatile main course lends itself to elegant entertaining
as well as to an informal gathering. To cut down on preparation time, have
your butcher bone and butterfly the leg of lamb when you purchase it.

4 garlic cloves

2 teaspoons fresh rosemary leaves

1 teaspoon whole black
  peppercorns

1 teaspoon salt

½ cup fresh mint leaves

2 tablespoons olive oil

2 tablespoons red wine vinegar

One 3½-pound trimmed &
  butterflied boneless leg of lamb

Garlic & Mint Aïoli:

1 garlic head, cloves
  separated & peeled

1 large egg

1½ tablespoons fresh lemon juice

1½ cups olive oil

½ cup fresh mint leaves, slivered

1 teaspoon fresh rosemary
  leaves, crumbled

½ teaspoon salt

Using a mortar and pestle, mash together the garlic, rosemary, peppercorns, salt, mint, olive oil, and vinegar until the mixture forms a paste. Rub the lamb all over with the mixture. Place the lamb in a roasting pan, cover with plastic wrap, and let stand at room temperature for 1 hour.

Prepare a fire in a kettle-type charcoal grill. When the coals are burning white, divide them into 2 parts and push them to either side of the grill. Place the grill rack over the coals and put the lamb, fat side down, in the center of the rack. Close the lid, leaving the vents open. Grill for about 30 minutes, or until a meat thermometer inserted into the thickest part of the meat registers 135°F. (The meat will range from rare in the thicker parts to medium in the thinner parts.) Transfer the

Grilled Leg of Lamb with Garlic and Mint Aïoli
& Couscous with Fruited Vegetable Sauce, page 40

lamb to a cutting board, cover loosely with foil, and let rest for 10 minutes.

Meanwhile, prepare the aïoli: Preheat the oven to 400°F. Wrap the garlic in foil and bake for about 30 minutes, or until soft. Let cool slightly.

In a food processor fitted with the metal blade, combine the egg and roasted garlic and process until pureed. In a small bowl, combine the lemon juice and oil. With the motor running, pour the oil mixture through the feed tube in a thin steady stream until combined. (The sauce will be the consistency of mayonnaise.) Transfer the sauce to a small bowl. Stir in the mint, rosemary, and salt.

Carve the lamb and serve with the aïoli on the side. **Serves 8.**

Endive and Blue Cheese Risotto with Walnuts

Here's the West Coast version of a classic Italian rice dish.
Risotto's creamy texture comes from Arborio rice, a short-grain rice that
can absorb more liquid ~ and more flavor ~ than other varieties.
It can be found in Italian markets and specialty food stores. When preparing
this recipe, it is important to use a good-quality chicken stock,
preferably homemade, for the best flavor. Serve the risotto on its own
or as an accompaniment to grilled meats or poultry.

1 tablespoon butter

1 tablespoon olive oil

*4 large leeks (about 2 pounds),
rinsed well & chopped
(white & tender green parts)*

*4 small Belgian endives
(about ½ pound), cut
crosswise into thin slices*

½ teaspoon salt, or to taste

½ teaspoon white pepper

5 to 6 cups chicken stock

2 cups Arborio rice

1 ounce blue cheese, crumbled

½ cup toasted chopped walnuts

In a large skillet, heat the butter and oil over medium heat. Add the leeks and cook over low heat, stirring occasionally, for about 20 minutes, or until the leeks are very soft. Add the endive, salt, and pepper. Cook, stirring occasionally, for about 10 minutes, or until the endive is very soft.

Meanwhile, in a medium-size saucepan, bring the chicken stock to a boil over high heat. Reduce the heat to low and keep the stock simmering.

Add the rice to the skillet and stir until well coated with butter. Cook, stirring frequently, for 5 minutes, or until the rice turns translucent. Add 2 cups of the simmering stock to the rice. Cook, over medium heat, stirring constantly, until all of the stock has been absorbed. Add 2½ cups more stock, ½ cup at

Joshua Tree National Monument

a time, adding more only when the previous amount has been absorbed; this should take about 20 minutes. The rice should be creamy and just tender.

Add the blue cheese and enough of the remaining stock to make the risotto creamy. Cook, stirring constantly, until the cheese is melted. Remove the pan from the heat. Stir in the walnuts and serve immediately. **Serves 6 to 8.**

California Pizza

Pizza is such a California favorite that even the best restaurants offer it with a dizzying and delicious array of toppings. This dough recipe will make 6 individual pizzas, but you don't have to bake all of them at once. Some of the dough can be punched down after it has risen, put in a plastic bag, and refrigerated until the next day. Just bring it to room temperature before using.

Pizza Dough:

1½ cups warm water

1 tablespoon active dry yeast

2 tablespoons olive oil

1½ teaspoons salt

4 cups all-purpose flour

Cornmeal, for sprinkling

Eggplant & Goat Cheese Topping:

1 large eggplant, cut crosswise into thin slices

3 tablespoons olive oil

3 ounces goat cheese, crumbled

½ cup sliced pitted black olives such as Kalamata

Salt & black pepper

Prepare the dough: In a food processor fitted with the metal blade, combine the water and yeast. Let stand for 5 minutes, or until the mixture begins to foam. Add the oil, salt, and 1 cup of the flour and process for 1 minute to blend. Add the remaining flour and process by pulsing on and off until the dough comes together in a ball. (The dough may be a little sticky; do not add more flour.)

Transfer the dough to a medium-size oiled bowl, turning to coat. Cover with plastic wrap and let rise in a warm place for about 1 hour, or until doubled in bulk.

Preheat the oven to 450°F. Lightly sprinkle 6 small pizza pans or 3 baking sheets with cornmeal. Unwrap the dough, punch it down, turn it out onto a work surface, and divide into 6 equal pieces. On a lightly floured surface, roll each piece of dough into a 6-inch round. Transfer the dough to the prepared pans.

Prepare the topping: Arrange 3 eggplant slices over each pizza and brush with 1½ teaspoons of the oil. Scatter the goat cheese and the olives over the eggplant. Sprinkle with salt and pepper to taste.

Let stand for 10 minutes, then bake for 15 minutes, or until the crust is golden. **Makes 6 individual pizzas.**

Chorizo & Red Bell Pepper Topping: In a medium-size skillet, heat 1 tablespoon olive oil over medium heat. Add 1½ cups red bell pepper strips and cook, stirring frequently, for 10 minutes, or until very soft. Add 3 ounces thinly sliced chorizo and cook, stirring frequently, for 2 minutes. Remove from the heat and drain off the excess oil. Thinly slice 2 large ripe tomatoes. Arrange the tomato slices over the pizzas. Spoon the pepper mixture over the tomatoes. Let stand for 10 minutes, then bake as directed above.

Shrimp Ravioli with Cilantro-Cream Pesto

With its Italian, Asian, and French influences, this pasta
dish exemplifies the culinary melting pot that is California cuisine.

1 recipe Basic Fresh Pasta
  Dough (p. 79)

Shrimp Filling:

2 scallions, chopped
  (white & tender green parts)

1 small carrot, peeled & chopped

One 1-inch piece ginger, peeled

¼ teaspoon hot-pepper flakes

¼ teaspoon salt

⅔ pound small shrimp, peeled

1 tablespoon Vietnamese or
  Thai fish sauce

½ cup heavy cream

Cilantro-Cream Pesto:

2 cups fresh cilantro leaves

3 small garlic cloves

One 1-inch piece ginger, peeled

2 teaspoons Asian sesame oil

½ teaspoon salt

½ cup heavy cream

Prepare the pasta dough and let rest, covered.

Prepare the filling: In a food processor fitted with the metal blade, combine the scallions, carrot, and ginger and process until finely chopped. Add the pepper flakes, salt, shrimp, fish sauce, and cream and process until well blended. Transfer to a medium-size bowl and set aside.

Prepare the pesto: In a food processor fitted with the metal blade, combine the cilantro, garlic, and ginger and process until finely chopped. Add the oil and salt and process to blend. With the motor running, add the cream through the feed tube and process until well blended. Transfer to a small bowl and set aside.

To assemble the ravioli, divide the pasta dough into quarters. On a floured surface, roll

out each piece of dough to a sheet about 6 inches wide and 24 inches long. Cut each sheet in half lengthwise.

Place mounds of the filling, about 1 tablespoon each, at 3-inch intervals down the center of one strip of pasta, leaving a 1-inch border at the top and bottom. Lightly brush the pasta with cold water around the mounds of filling. Cover with another strip of pasta, and press the sheets together around each mound of filling to seal. Using a pizza wheel or knife, cut the pasta into 3-inch squares. Repeat with the remaining ingredients. (You should have 32 ravioli.)

Bring a large saucepan of salted water to a boil over high heat. Cook the ravioli in the boiling water for 5 minutes, or until al dente; drain well.

To serve, divide the ravioli among 6 pasta bowls or plates and drizzle with the pesto. **Serves 6**.

California Winter Pasta

This is a hearty, homey dish, perfect to share with friends. Sweet Italian sausage is used in the sauce, but if you prefer, turkey sausage can be substituted.

2 tablespoons olive oil

¾ pound sweet Italian
   sausage links

3 garlic cloves, minced

1 (9-ounce) package frozen
   artichoke hearts, thawed

1 pound ripe tomatoes, peeled,
   seeded & chopped, or 1
   (16-ounce) can whole
   tomatoes in juice, chopped

Salt & black pepper

8 ounces small pitted black olives

1 pound dried rigatoni

8 ounces Camembert cheese

In a large skillet, heat the oil over medium-high heat. Add the sausages and cook, turning occasionally, for 5 minutes, or until lightly browned on all sides. Add the garlic and cook, stirring frequently, for 2 minutes. Add the artichoke hearts and cook, stirring frequently, for 3 minutes.

Remove the sausages to a cutting board. Reduce the heat to medium and add the tomatoes with their juice. Cut the sausages into ½-inch slices and add to the skillet. Cook, stirring occasionally, for 5 minutes, or until the sauce thickens slightly. Season to taste with the salt and pepper. Stir in the olives. Remove the skillet from the heat and keep warm.

Cook the rigatoni in a large saucepan of boiling water for 8 to 10 minutes, or until al dente; drain in a colander.

To serve, transfer the rigatoni to a large shallow bowl. Pinch off walnut-size pieces of cheese and add to the pasta. Add the sauce and toss for 30 seconds, or until the cheese is melted. Serve immediately. **Serves 6.**

The Old Town mission, San Diego

Polenta Lasagne

This California adaptation of an Italian classic makes
delicious use of the state's rich bounty of vegetables and adds a new twist
to traditional lasagne. Polenta, a northern Italian favorite, is
the name for both coarsely ground cornmeal and a dish made from that cornmeal
cooked in water or stock until thick and creamy.

Vegetable Layer:

2 to 3 tablespoons olive oil

1 medium eggplant, unpeeled,
  cut crosswise into ½-inch slices

1 teaspoon salt

2 medium red bell peppers,
  seeded & cut lengthwise into
  8 strips each

1 medium onion, cut into
  ½-inch slices

2 medium zucchini, cut
  lengthwise into ½-inch slices

White Sauce:

2 tablespoons unsalted butter

1 tablespoon all-purpose flour

1¼ cups milk

¼ teaspoon salt

¼ teaspoon white pepper

Pinch of grated nutmeg

Polenta Layer:

6 cups water

1 tablespoon salt

2 cups polenta

1 cup milk

1 cup grated aged Asiago
  or Parmesan cheese

4 ounces smoked or plain
  mozzarella cheese, shredded

Prepare the vegetables: Heat a large skillet or griddle over medium-high heat. Add 1 tablespoon of olive oil, swirling to coat the bottom of the skillet. Add the eggplant, sprinkle with the salt, and cook, turning occasionally, for 8 to 10 minutes, or until the eggplant softens

and begins to brown. Remove the eggplant to a shallow bowl. Add 1 tablespoon of olive oil to the skillet. Add the peppers and onion and cook, stirring occasionally, for 8 to 10 minutes, or until the vegetables soften and begin to brown. Remove to the bowl with the eggplant. Add more oil to the skillet, then add the zucchini and cook, turning occasionally, for 8 to 10 minutes, or until it softens and begins to brown. Add to the eggplant mixture.

Prepare the sauce: In a small saucepan, melt the butter over medium heat. Add the flour and cook, stirring constantly, for 2 minutes. Add the milk all at once and cook, stirring constantly, for 3 to 4 minutes, or until slightly thickened. Stir in the salt, pepper, and nutmeg. Remove the pan from the heat and set aside.

Prepare the polenta: In a large saucepan, bring the water and salt to a boil over high heat. Gradually stir in the polenta. Reduce the heat to medium and cook, stirring constantly with a wooden spoon, for 15 minutes. (The mixture will become quite thick.) Add the milk and Asiago cheese and cook, stirring frequently, for 5 minutes, or until smooth and creamy.

Pour half the polenta into a 9-by-12-inch baking dish. Using the back of a spoon, smooth the polenta evenly over the bottom of the dish. Transfer the remaining polenta to the top of a double boiler and keep warm over barely simmering water.

Preheat the oven to 400°F. Coarsely chop the sautéed vegetables. Spread them over the polenta layer. Spoon the remaining polenta over the vegetables, covering them completely and smoothing the top. Let stand for 5 minutes to firm.

Pour the sauce over the polenta, spreading it evenly with the back of a spoon. Sprinkle the mozzarella evenly over the top. Bake for 45 minutes, or until golden brown and bubbly. Let stand for 5 to 10 minutes before cutting. **Serves 8**.

Basic Fresh Pasta Dough

Silken strands of fresh pasta lightly coated with sauce,
or pillows of fresh pasta stuffed with an imaginative filling, make
an elegant first course or light main course.

2 cups all-purpose flour
1 teaspoon salt

3 large eggs
1 tablespoon olive oil

In a food processor fitted with the metal blade, combine all the ingredients and process until the dough holds together. Gather the dough into a ball, cover with a kitchen towel, and let rest for 30 minutes.

Alternatively, in a large bowl, combine the flour and salt. Make a well in the center of the mixture. In a small bowl, combine the eggs and oil. Pour the mixture into the well and mix with a wooden spoon until well blended. Turn the dough out onto a lightly floured surface and knead for 5 to 8 minutes, or until smooth and elastic. Cover with a kitchen towel and let rest for 30 minutes. The pasta can be refrigerated, wrapped in plastic, for up to 1 week. **Makes about 1 pound.**

Grilled Radicchio and Goat Cheese Pasta Roll

When sliced, the filling for this elegant pasta roll creates a stylish spiral.
Because it can be assembled ahead, it's great for a dinner party.

½ recipe Basic Fresh Pasta
  Dough (p. 79)

Radicchio & Goat Cheese Filling:

2 small heads radicchio (about ½
  pound), cut in half

1 tablespoon olive oil

4 ounces cream cheese, softened

4 ounces soft mild goat cheese

1 cup grated aged Asiago or
  Parmesan cheese

2 large eggs

Salt & black pepper

Creamy Balsamic Sauce:

⅓ cup balsamic vinegar

12 small fresh sage leaves, chopped

⅔ cup unsalted butter, chilled

Salt & black pepper

Prepare the pasta dough according to the recipe and let rest, covered, for 30 minutes.

Prepare the filling: Place the radicchio in a shallow bowl, sprinkle with the oil, and turn to coat.

Heat a large heavy skillet over medium-high heat. Add the radicchio and cook, turning occasionally, for about 3 minutes, or until it wilts and the outside leaves begin to brown. Transfer to a cutting board and coarsely chop.

In a large bowl, combine the cream cheese, goat cheese, Asiago, and eggs and stir until smooth and well blended. Stir in the radicchio. Season to taste with salt and pepper. Set aside.

Divide the pasta dough into 6 equal pieces. On a floured surface, roll 1 piece of dough into a thin sheet approximately 4½ by 11 inches. Lightly flour a kitchen towel, and place the sheet of pasta on the towel. Roll out another piece of dough and place it on the towel so one

of the long edges overlaps the first sheet by 1 inch. Repeat with a third piece of dough. (You will have a sheet of pasta approximately 11 inches square.)

Spread half the filling over the dough, leaving a 1-inch border around the edges. Using the towel as a guide, roll the pasta up over the filling into a tight cylinder. Cut a piece of cheesecloth approximately 12 by 10 inches. Tightly roll the pasta up in the cheesecloth. Tie the ends of the cheesecloth with kitchen string. Repeat with the remaining ingredients, and roll up the second roll in cheesecloth.

Bring a large saucepan or stockpot of salted water to a boil. Carefully add the pasta rolls to the water and cook for 20 minutes. (It's all right if the pasta rolls are curled a little to fit into the pan.) Drain. When the pasta rolls are cool enough to handle, unwrap them and discard the cheesecloth. (The pasta rolls can be prepared up to this point,

cooled completely, and refrigerated, covered in plastic wrap, for up to 3 days.)

Preheat the oven to 350°F. Cut the pasta rolls into ½-inch slices and lay flat on an ungreased baking sheet or in a baking pan. Cover loosely with foil and bake for about 20 minutes (35 minutes if chilled), or until heated through.

Meanwhile, prepare the sauce: In a small heavy skillet, combine the vinegar and sage and bring to a boil over high heat. Boil for 3 minutes, or until the vinegar is reduced to 2 tablespoons. Reduce the heat to low and gradually whisk in the chilled butter, 1 tablespoon at a time, until the sauce is thick and creamy. Remove the pan from the heat and season to taste with salt and pepper.

Arrange the pasta slices on individual serving plates. Drizzle the sauce over the slices and serve immediately. **Serves 6.**

Chocolate Almond Torte
with White Chocolate

An easy way to make a dark chocolate cake look especially intriguing is to splatter melted white chocolate over it. This decadent, eye-catching torte will make a dramatic conclusion to the most elegant dinner.

Chocolate Almond Torte:

1 cup blanched whole almonds

6 ounces semisweet chocolate chips (1 cup)

½ cup (1 stick) unsalted butter, softened

⅔ cup sugar

3 large eggs

¼ cup dry bread crumbs

2 tablespoons grated orange zest

Chocolate Glaze:

¼ cup (½ stick) unsalted butter

2 ounces unsweetened chocolate, chopped

3 ounces semisweet chocolate chips (½ cup)

2 tablespoons light corn syrup

White Chocolate Decoration:

3 ounces white chocolate, chopped

2 teaspoons solid vegetable shortening

Prepare the torte: Preheat the oven to 350°F. Grease an 8-inch round cake pan and line the bottom with parchment or waxed paper.

In a food processor fitted with the metal blade, process the almonds until finely chopped. Set aside.

Melt the chocolate chips in the top of a double boiler set over barely simmering (not boiling) water, stirring until smooth. Remove the chocolate from the water and set aside to cool slightly.

In a large bowl, cream together the butter

and sugar. Add the eggs one at a time, beating well after each addition. Add the bread crumbs, melted chocolate, chopped almonds, and orange zest, and beat until just combined.

Scrape the batter into the prepared pan and smooth the surface. Bake for 30 to 35 minutes, or until the top is cracked and the torte has pulled away from the sides of the pan. Set the pan on a wire rack to cool for 30 minutes.

Prepare the glaze: In a small saucepan, melt the butter over medium-low heat. Add both chocolates and stir until melted and smooth. Add the corn syrup and stir until the glaze is smooth and satiny. Remove the pan from the heat and let cool for about 5 minutes, or until thickened slightly.

Turn the cake out onto a rack, peel off the paper, and set the rack over a baking sheet. Pour the glaze over the torte and, using a long metal spatula, smooth it evenly over the top and sides. Let stand for 15 minutes, or until the glaze is set.

To decorate, melt the white chocolate with the shortening in the top of a double boiler set over barely simmering (not boiling) water, stirring until smooth. Using a fork, splatter the white chocolate over the top of the torte, working in several different directions. Let the torte stand for at least 1 hour at room temperature to firm before serving. **Serves 8 to 10.**

Filo Purses Stuffed with Caramelized Apples and Walnuts

Crisp on the outside and meltingly sweet on the inside, these filo (or phyllo) purse-shaped pouches are elegant and festive but surprisingly easy to make. Be sure to keep the sheets of filo covered with plastic wrap, as the dough dries out easily.

7 tablespoons unsalted butter

5 large cooking apples such as Granny Smith, peeled, cored & cut into ¼-inch slices

1 cup sugar

1 cup walnut pieces

8 sheets frozen filo dough, thawed

Confectioners' sugar, for dusting (optional)

In a medium-size skillet, melt 4 tablespoons of the butter over medium heat. Add the apples and cook, stirring frequently, for 3 minutes, or until they begin to soften. Add the sugar and cook, stirring frequently, for 3 minutes more, or until the apples are soft but not mushy. Remove the apples with a slotted spoon to a plate. Set aside.

Cook the syrup remaining in the skillet for 3 to 4 minutes, or until it just begins to caramelize. Add the walnuts and cook, stirring frequently, until they are well coated and the syrup has darkened slightly. Add the walnuts and syrup to the apples. Set aside.

Preheat the oven to 400°F. Lightly butter a baking sheet. Cut eight 12-by-1-inch strips from a sheet of foil.

In a small saucepan, melt the remaining 3 tablespoons of butter over medium heat. Place 1 sheet of filo on a work surface and, using a pastry brush, lightly brush with melted butter. Fold the sheet in half crosswise to form a square. Lightly brush with more melted butter. Put ⅓ cup of the apple

mixture in the middle of the square. Gather the 4 corners of the filo over the filling to form a purse. Wrap a strip of foil around the neck of the purse and pinch the foil together to tie it, letting the ends of the foil hang free. Transfer to the prepared baking sheet. Repeat with the remaining filo and filling.

Bake the purses for about 30 minutes, or until golden and crisp. Set on a wire rack to cool slightly. Remove the foil strips. Generously sift confectioners' sugar over the purses, if desired, then transfer to individual serving plates. **Serves 8**.

Sourdough Bread Pudding with Orange Muscat Wine Sauce

Sourdough bread and dried fruits add a California twist to a favorite old-fashioned dessert. Both the pudding and sauce are flavored with orange muscat, an aromatic dessert wine with a slightly spicy flavor.

Sourdough Bread Pudding:

½ cup orange muscat wine or brandy

½ cup raisins

¼ cup chopped pitted prunes

¼ cup chopped dried apricots

⅔ cup granulated sugar

8 slices day-old sourdough bread, about ½ inch thick, crusts removed

3 tablespoons unsalted butter, melted

2½ cups milk

3 large eggs, lightly beaten

1 teaspoon pure vanilla extract

Orange Muscat Wine Sauce:

1½ cups orange muscat wine or brandy

½ cup (1 stick) unsalted butter, softened

1 cup confectioners' sugar

1 large egg

1 tablespoon grated orange zest

Prepare the pudding: In a small nonreactive saucepan, heat the wine over medium heat until hot but not boiling. Remove the pan from the heat and stir in the raisins, prunes, and apricots. Set aside.

In a medium-size heavy skillet, cook the granulated sugar, stirring frequently, over medium-high heat until it caramelizes and turns a deep gold color. Carefully pour the melted sugar into an 8-inch round baking pan, swirling the pan to coat the bottom and sides evenly.

41--GOLDEN GATE BRIDGE SPANNING THE GOLDEN GATE
SAN FRANCISCO TO MARIN COUNTY, CALIFORNIA

Cover the bottom of the prepared pan with the bread slices. Drizzle the melted butter over the bread.

In a medium-size bowl, combine the milk, eggs, vanilla, and the soaked dried fruits with the wine. Pour the mixture over the bread. Let stand at room temperature for 30 minutes.

Preheat the oven to 350°F. Put the bread pudding into a larger baking pan and fill the baking pan with enough hot water to come halfway up the sides of the pudding. Bake the pudding in the water bath for 1 hour, or until firm.

Meanwhile, prepare the sauce: In a medium-size nonreactive saucepan, boil the wine over high heat for 4 minutes, or until reduced by half. Set aside.

In a small bowl, using an electric mixer set at medium speed, cream together the butter and confectioners' sugar until light and fluffy. Beat in the egg and orange zest. Whisk this mixture into the reduced wine. Cook over low heat, stirring constantly, for 4 minutes, or until the sauce thickens slightly. (The sauce can be made ahead and set aside at room temperature for 2 to 4 hours. Reheat over low heat just before serving.)

Remove the pudding from the water bath and let stand for 10 minutes. Run a knife around the edge of the pudding to loosen it from the sides of the pan. Invert a serving plate over the pudding, then invert the pudding onto the plate. Serve with the warm sauce. **Serves 6.**

Fresh Figs Poached in Red Wine with Mascarpone

The fig was brought to California by Spanish missionaries in the 16th century, and today over 95 percent of all figs grown in the United States come from California. The rich but mild mascarpone, a creamy Italian cheese, is available in gourmet shops and some supermarkets.

2 cups dry California red wine such as cabernet sauvignon, or 1 cup wine & 1 cup water

2 cups sugar

Two 3-inch cinnamon sticks

1 teaspoon mixed peppercorns (black, white, pink, green)

2 whole cloves

18 fresh figs

1 cup mascarpone

In a medium-size nonreactive saucepan, combine the wine, sugar, cinnamon sticks, peppercorns, and cloves. Bring to a boil over high heat. Reduce the heat to medium-low and simmer, uncovered, for 15 minutes.

Add the figs to the syrup in a single layer, reduce the heat to low, and cook, covered, over low heat for 30 minutes. Remove the pan from the heat and let the figs cool in the syrup.

Transfer the cooled figs with the syrup to a medium bowl, cover with plastic wrap, and chill for at least 8 hours, or up to 5 days.

To serve, remove the figs from the syrup, reserving the syrup, and cut off the stem ends. Arrange 3 figs in the center of each individual serving plate. Spoon the mascarpone into a pastry bag fitted with a small star tip and pipe a rosette of mascarpone on top of each fig. Or, using a small spoon, put a dollop of the mascarpone on each fig. Spoon the syrup around the figs. **Serves 6**.

Adobo sauce: A thick Mexican sauce made from ground chiles, vinegar, and herbs that is commonly used to flavor soups. In the United States it is usually sold canned with chiles chipotles.

Aïoli: A garlic mayonnaise that originated in the Provence region of France. It is used as a sauce for meat, fish, and vegetables.

Artichoke: This globe-shaped vegetable is the bud of a thistlelike plant that is harvested before it blooms. Small young artichokes are tender enough to eat whole; large ones have a fuzzy interior choke that must be removed. Artichokes are grown primarily along California's central coast.

Arugula: Also known as rocket, rugola, and Italian cress, this delicate salad green has slender dark leaves with a slightly bitter, peppery flavor.

Asiago cheese: A semifirm yellow Italian cheese with a nutty flavor. Aged Asiago is suitable for grating and can be used as a table cheese.

Belgian endive: Also known as French endive and witloof, Belgian endive is the blanched shoots of the chicory root (grown in darkness to prevent them from turning green). They are 4 to 6 inches long, with tightly packed white-yellow leaves and a slightly bitter flavor. Endive is usually used raw in salads or cooked by braising or boiling.

Chile peppers: Members of the *Capsicum* genus, chiles come in all shapes, sizes, and colors, ranging from fiery hot to mild. There are hundreds of different types of chiles grown in hot or tropical climates throughout the world. They are sold fresh, dried, crushed, canned, and in powdered form. The seeds and veins are the hottest parts and can be irritating to the skin; be sure to wear rubber gloves when handling them. The following are five popular types of chiles:

> **Ancho:** Dark reddish-brown dried peppers, about 4 inches long and 2 inches wide, with a mild flavor. In its fresh form the ancho is called a poblano.
>
> **Chile chipotle:** Dried smoked peppers related to the jalapeño pepper. They are most commonly sold canned in adobo sauce.
>
> **Guajillo:** Slender dried peppers, about 4 inches long, with a smooth dark red skin. They are extremely hot and very flavorful.
>
> **Jalapeño:** Dark green and plump, about 2 inches long and ranging from hot to very hot. They're popular in cooking because they are easily seeded.
>
> **Serrano:** Small bullet-shaped peppers about 1½ inches long and extremely hot. As they mature, the dark green skin turns an orange-red color.

Chorizo: A spicy sausage made with pork (either fresh or smoked), garlic, ground chiles, and other spices. It is used extensively in both Latin American and Spanish cooking.

Coriander: This herb was once grown only in the Mediterranean region but is now cultivated worldwide. The leaves of the plant, also known as cilantro or Chinese parsley, resemble flat-leaf parsley and are used fresh; the seeds are dried and used either whole or ground.

Dungeness crab: Named after the town of Dungeness on Washington's Olympic Peninsula, where it was first commercially harvested, this large hard-shelled crab can weigh as much as 4 pounds. It has a slightly sweet and succulent flavor and is a very popular food on the West Coast.

Eggs: All recipes calling for raw egg, such as mayonnaise, aïoli, and Caesar salad dressing, should be consumed or refrigerated immediately to decrease the risk of salmonella. Covered and stored in the refrigerator, dishes containing raw eggs can last up to 3 days.

Filo: Also spelled "phyllo," filo is a wheat-flour dough rolled into tissue-thin sheets. When brushed with butter and baked, it becomes crisp and flaky. Filo is often used as a wrapper for sweet and savory fillings, especially in Greek and Middle Eastern cooking.

Flying fish roe: The tiny eggs of the flying fish have a bright orange color, crunchy texture, and strong fishy flavor.

Frisée: A member of the chicory family, this lettuce has pale green curly leaves, a sturdy crisp texture, and a distinctive bittersweet taste.

Goat cheese: Also called chèvre, goat's milk cheese has a tangy, slightly sour flavor. Young goat cheese is mild and creamy; aged goat cheese becomes drier and stronger in flavor.

Hoisin sauce: A thick reddish-brown sauce made from soybeans, garlic, chiles, and spices. It has a sweet and spicy flavor and is used in Chinese cooking as a flavoring and as a condiment.

Linguiça: A long, thin smoked Portuguese sausage made from pork, garlic, and paprika.

Mascarpone cheese: A rich, buttery Italian cheese made from cow's milk. It has a texture similar to cream cheese and mild flavor and is often sweetened and used in desserts.

Mustard greens: These sturdy cooking greens are the leaves of the mustard plant. They are best eaten when young and tender—their appealing bite can become very sharp as the leaves get larger.

Nori: Seaweed that is dried, pressed, cut into thin sheets, and usually toasted. It is used as an edible wrap for sushi or finely shredded as a garnish.

Extra-virgin olive oil: Made from the first pressing of the olives, this fruity oil is considered one of the finest because it has an acid level of less than 1%. California is a major producer.

Potatoes: Because they are hardy and easy to grow, these tubers are one of the world's most important food crops. There are hundreds of varieties cultivated worldwide:

> **Blue:** Included in this category are Blue Carib and All Blue. They have a grayish-blue skin and dark blue flesh. Mild and delicate in flavor, they are best boiled.
>
> **German Fingerling:** Small light-skinned potatoes with a lumpy shape and yellow, waxy flesh. They are best boiled whole.
>
> **New:** The young small potatoes of any variety. They have a slightly sweet, mild flavor and tender skin and are best steamed or boiled whole.
>
> **Purple:** Grown in Peru, these small to medium-size potatoes have a dark purple skin and bright purple flesh. Similar to russets, they are good baked or mashed.

Yellow Finn: Grown in Washington State, these golden-skinned potatoes have a creamy yellow flesh and a buttery flavor. This variety is good to use in potato salads and for mashing.

Yukon Gold: Medium-size yellow-skinned potatoes with a slightly sweet flavor and a smooth, moist texture. Yukon Golds are good steamed, boiled, or baked.

Radicchio: A member of the chicory family, radicchio is a small head of loosely packed burgundy-red leaves with white veins. The leaves have a slightly bitter flavor. Radicchio is used raw in salads and often grilled, sautéed, or braised.

Saffron threads: These dried stigmas of the saffron crocus have a vivid orange-yellow color and pungent aromatic flavor. They are used to color food as well as to flavor it. Because the stigmas are hand-picked, this spice is the most expensive in the world.

Sesame oil: Extracted from sesame seeds, this oil has a strong nutty flavor. It is used sparingly as a flavoring in Chinese, Korean, and Japanese cuisine.

Shiitake mushrooms: Also known as black forest mushrooms, these wild mushrooms have large brown meaty caps, thin stalks, and an earthy, smoky flavor. They are sold both fresh and dried. Once grown only in Japan, they have recently been cultivated in the United States.

Swiss chard: This hardy green, with its crinkly dark leaves and white stems, is a member of the beet family. When cooked, the leaves become sweet and silky. The crisp celerylike stems can be cooked separately.

Thai fish sauce: A thin dark sauce with a strong fish flavor that is used extensively in Asian cooking as a flavoring and as a condiment. It is also called Vietnamese fish sauce.

Tomatoes: Fresh tomatoes are available year round in supermarkets, but vine-ripened ones, which are superior in flavor, are available only in the summer and fall. Hydroponic (grown in water) and hothouse tomatoes look appealing but generally lack flavor. Greenmarkets now offer a wide range of tomatoes, including some historic varieties that are being reintroduced by specialty producers:

Caro Rich: Medium-size orange tomatoes with a rich flavor and a good acid and sugar balance.

Currant: Red or yellow currant-size tomatoes that grow in clusters. Visually spectacular in salads and as a plate garnish.

Fakel: Large red, juicy tomatoes with excellent flavor, often used in salads.

Lemon Boy: A new hybrid slightly larger than a baseball with a bright yellow color.

Sun-dried: Sliced tomatoes that are dried in the sun or in a dehydrator, then dry-packed or packed in olive oil. Dark red with a rich, concentrated flavor, they are used in salads, sauces, and many cooked dishes.

Sweet 100: Very small, intensely flavored red cherry tomatoes, best used whole in salads and as garnishes.

Yellow Pear: Small pear-shaped tomatoes with a mild flavor used in salads and for eating out of hand.

Wasabi: Called Japanese horseradish because of its edible root and sharp pungent flavor, wasabi is generally available in paste and powdered form. It is used to flavor sushi, and is mixed with soy sauce as a condiment with many Japanese-style dishes.

WEIGHTS

OUNCES AND POUNDS	METRICS
¼ ounce	7 grams
⅓ ounce	10 grams
½ ounce	14 grams
1 ounce	28 grams
1½ ounces	42 grams
1¾ ounces	50 grams
2 ounces	57 grams
3 ounces	85 grams
3½ ounces	100 grams
4 ounces (¼ pound)	114 grams
6 ounces	170 grams
8 ounces (½ pound)	227 grams
9 ounces	250 grams
16 ounces (1 pound)	464 grams

LIQUID MEASURES

tsp.: teaspoon
Tbs.: tablespoon

SPOONS AND CUPS	METRIC EQUIVALENTS
¼ tsp.	1.23 milliliters
½ tsp.	2.5 milliliters
¾ tsp.	3.7 milliliters
1 tsp.	5 milliliters
1 dessertspoon	10 milliliters
1 Tbs. (3 tsp.)	15 milliliters
2 Tbs. (1 ounce)	30 milliliters
¼ cup	60 milliliters
⅓ cup	80 milliliters
½ cup	120 milliliters
⅔ cup	160 milliliters
¾ cup	180 milliliters
1 cup (8 ounces)	240 milliliters
2 cups (1 pint)	480 milliliters
3 cups	720 milliliters
4 cups (1 quart)	1 liter
4 quarts (1 gallon)	3¾ liters

TEMPERATURES

°F (FAHRENHEIT)	°C (CENTIGRADE OR CELSIUS)
32 (water freezes)	0
200	95
212 (water boils)	100
250	120
275	135
300 (slow oven)	150
325	160
350 (moderate oven)	175
375	190
400 (hot oven)	205
425	220
450 (very hot oven)	232
475	245
500 (extremely hot oven)	260

LENGTH

U.S. MEASUREMENTS	METRIC EQUIVALENTS
⅛ inch	3mm
¼ inch	6mm
⅜ inch	1 cm
½ inch	1.2 cm
¾ inch	2 cm
1 inch	2.5 cm
1¼ inches	3.1 cm
1½ inches	3.7 cm
2 inches	5 cm
3 inches	7.5 cm
4 inches	10 cm
5 inches	12.5 cm

APPROXIMATE EQUIVALENTS

1 kilo is slightly more than 2 pounds
1 liter is slightly more than 1 quart
1 meter is slightly over 3 feet
1 centimeter is approximately ⅜ inch

INDEX